except

by

nature

THE NATIONAL POETRY SERIES

The National Poetry Series was established in 1978 to ensure the publication of five poetry collections annually through participating publishers. Publication is funded by James A. Michener, The Copernicus Society of America, Edward J. Piszek, The Lannan Foundation, and the Tiny Tiger Foundation.

1997 COMPETITION WINNERS

SANDRA ALCOSSER
Except by Nature
Chosen by Eamon Grennan
Published by Graywolf Press

MARTINE BELLEN
Tales of Murasaki and Other Poems
Chosen by Rosmarie Waldrop
Published by Sun & Moon Press

ROBERT GIBB
The Origins of Evening
Chosen by Eavan Boland
Published by W.W. Norton

LISA LEWIS
Silent Treatment
Chosen by Stanley Plumly
Published by Penguin Books

HEATHER RAMSDELL
Lost Wax
Chosen by James Tate
Published by University of Illinois Press

Whether immersed in the exotic claustrophobia and sexual edginess of a Louisiana bayou ("mushed together and sticky as gumbo"), or smelling again the sweat of workers in her father's garage ("they torqued lugnets, flipped fag ends / into gravel"), or remembering an aunt's passion for extravagant hats ("the velvet inkpots of Schiaparelli, the mousseline de soie of Lilly Daché"), or simply feeling the strangeness of "a wild mallard in my palm / hoodlum heart whooping like a blood balloon," Sandra Alcosser always gives us poems vivid with what she calls "the tangible feel / of being alive." Vitality, zest, gusto mark all her responses to a world which—as she sees it from her own bright, original angle—never stops "jittering with possibility." In a language that enhances lyricism with judgement, enriches philosophic response with the cadences of exhilaration and surprise, she can at once affirm and interrogate the material, meaning, and value of her experience.

I love the buoyant verbal manners of these poems, which bring politeness and ecstasy into curious alignments, and which—without betrayal—transform the plain facts of life into fixtures of radiance. Such surfaces and muscular rhythms consistently testify to how well Alcosser has learned her trade.

In one poem Alcosser describes Carnival as "a fugitive stage of rapture," and her imagination strikes me as always having something of Carnival in it, tempered by an honest consciousness that is no stranger to the more sobering actualities of Lent. There is, too, something of the chameleon in her work, as if she'd taken Keats's notion of "negative capability" to heart, and given it a distinct feminist spin: "Perhaps we both are lost in our landscape, / woman and chameleon always changing to save our skin." Add to this the intense empathy of her responses in different poems to a wildcat, a hermit thrush, a squirrel, a duck, a woodpecker, grizzly bears, and a spittle bug, and you have an imagination eager to see and spell out not only the ways in which it can inhabit the world, but the even more colorful ways it can be in-formed and in-habited by the world.

Except by Nature is an exceptional collection: feisty, accomplished, and mature; its poems (and some fine prose poems, strange little fables sprouting from the ordinary ground of reminiscence) brim with serious delights. It's a pleasure to usher them into the world.

EAMON GRENNAN

except

by

nature

Sandra Alcosser

GRAYWOLF

PRESS

Publication of this volume is made possible in part by a grant
provided by the Minnesota State Arts Board through an appro-
priation by the Minnesota State Legislature, and by a grant from
the National Endowment for the Arts. Significant support has
also been provided by Dayton's, Mervyn's, and Target stores
through the Dayton Hudson Foundation, the Andrew W. Mellon
Foundation, the McKnight Foundation, the General Mills
Foundation, the St. Paul Companies, and other generous contri-
butions from foundations, corporations, and individuals. To
these organizations and individuals we offer our heartfelt thanks.

Published by Graywolf Press
2402 University Avenue, Suite 203
Saint Paul, Minnesota 55114
All rights reserved.

www.graywolfpress.org

Published in the United States of America

ISBN 1-55597-273-X

2 4 6 8 9 7 5 3 1
First Graywolf Printing, 1998

Library of Congress Catalog Card Number: 97-80078

Cover photograph:
Clyde Butcher, "Amelia Island," 1989

Cover design:
Jeanne Lee

Acknowledgments

These poems appeared, sometimes in different versions, in the following journals and anthologies to whose editors I am grateful:

The American Poetry Review: "Azaleas"
The Bloomsbury Review: "Thirst "
Columbia: A Magazine of Prose and Poetry: "Worms" and "Pole Boat, Honey Island"
CutBank: "He Paints the Kingdom of Decay: His Goddess Escapes," "The Stray Sod,"
    and "Throughout the Duration of a Pulse a Heart Changes Form"
The Indiana Review: "Flame"
Mañoa: "Glory Monster" and "Spittle Bug"
The Michigan Quarterly Review: "The Intricacy of the Song Inverse to the Dull Lores"
Nimrod: "The Anatomy of Air" and "Rags"
The North American Review: "Woodpecker"
Northern Lights: "Approaching August" and "What Makes the Grizzlies Dance"
Orion Magazine: "Trajectory" and "Wildcat Path"
The Pacific Review: "Greenhand"
Ploughshares: "Skiing by Moonlight"
Poetry: "In Case of Rapture This Taxi Will Explode"
University Press of New England: Introspections: "By the Nape"
The Women's Review of Books: "Dancing the Tarantella at the County Farm"
    and "In the Jittering World"
The Yale Review: "Michael's Wine"

ANTHOLOGIES: *Imaginary Animals,* Harry Abrams Publication, 1997; *Something in Common,* Louisiana State University Press, Baton Rouge, 1998; *Poems for a Small Planet: Bread Loaf Quarterly / New England Review Anthology of Nature Poetry,* 1993; *Pushcart Prize Edition VIII,* Penguin, 1989; *The Forgotten Language: Contemporary Poets and Nature,* Peregrine Smith Books, 1991; *Constructing Nature,* Prentice-Hall, 1996; *Northern Lights,* Vintage Books, Random House, 1994; *Windows on the World,* World Wildlife Fund, 1997

BRIGHTON PRESS: a fine arts collaboration of three poems from this manuscript with Michele Burgess and Bill Kelly, 1992

THE PROSE PIECES that introduce the second and third sections were prepared for: *Causing Each Tentative Voice to Speak,* AWP Chronicle, 1989; and *The Erotic Life of Subdivisions: Sustaining the Wild in Wilderness,* The Cinnabar Symposium, Bozeman, Montana, 1994.

I also wish to express gratitude to the National Endowment for the Arts, The Montana Arts Council, The San Diego Arts Council, The University of Michigan, and San Diego State University for their support.

And to my family, Philip Maechling, The Rattlesnake Ladies Salon, and the fine poets of Wildcat Road, thank you.

Contents

By the Nape

except

by

nature

My Number

I'm linked with the fate of the world's disasters and only
have a little freedom to live or die
VÎTESLAV NEZVAL

My number is small. A hundred pounds of water,
A quart of salt. Her digit is a garment.

I wear her like a shadow. We judge each other,
My number and I. She is the title. The license.

The cash drawer. My random number.
She protects me from myself. She desires me.

She says she's only one of thirty million species.
She wishes she were more than anecdotal evidence.

Being human she can erect elaborate scaffolding
To protect her emotions, can make an excuse of obvious

Dramatic proportions. My number is inconsequential
With dreams of glory. She spends three or four days each year

Just opening her mail. Do you know how many animals
Will be given lethal injections while you read this poem.

Five billion people = half a billion empty bellies.
If there is a god, why can't that god be smaller than my number,

Tiny, soft-spoken so she'd have to pay attention.
My number is a female impersonator (she has multiple meanings).

Her shape is misleading. The further she is from unity, the more deeply
Involved with the world. Like the winds and the grasses, she wears herself down.

She lies under hot flags of lilies, sings like a bee.
She gets so lonely she recites for her cat. She makes her face up

Like a death mask. She hangs her dresses on the clothesline outside.
Together we dance—my number and her best dresses.

Sugary Heat

Dream and fester. The potential for evil and irrational growth. So the tropics with their perfume and juice threatened to consume. Antediluvian world in suspension. A visitor— I had no social order, no mythology to save the mind. My native friends cultivated a madness of operatic proportion, writing letters in menstrual blood, inviting me to discuss philosophy while we drank champagne on immaculate white beds. Their antebellum homes, between refineries and factories, each had a bridge to the Mississippi lit by small lights, like the entrance to Disneyland, Tinkerbell illuminating slippery chutes and stacks. Devil's Swamp. Alligator Bayou. I floated the Atchafalaya, snakes sliding down beside me, until my mind became baptized. Stained.

Pole Boat at Honey Island

The way he pushes deeper
into everything I hate—the heat rising
like wet crepe from silt and muck
to fill our lungs with its rotten breath.

Listen to the grunting armadillos
pad the tule pond on tiny feet.
Listen to the owl croon
in the loblolly.

I want to be brave, to bathe
myself in the humid night,
to cross the irradiant lawn
under magnolias,

those creamy-faced babies
perched in evergreen leaves,
to float through dives,
sick-smelling bayous full of turtle,

yellow-capped night heron,
to let the air penetrate at last,
the miasma that sends women to attics,
sets them scratching walls like mice,

rocking, humming with no release.
But I am afraid. I have danced
the sad slippers. I have placed
a hand on blind branches,

felt it flame with fire ants.
My lover's body like water snakes,
his sweat the odor of crawfish,
boiled. As he poles deeper

into the gauzy night—water swims
beside kerosene. So too as peepers

fill their bugle pouches—
like voices in an asylum,

an orchestra of cracked reeds,
throbbing sacs of chameleon—
we strum our giddy throats.
We begin to screech.

Azaleas

Sisters climb the bedroom window, lay themselves on the night table like pink fish, like negligees and soap slivers, diaphanous, pale veined. Wrapped through doors, leopard-spotted nectar paths pour down a wash of purple stars. I remember women in New Orleans, some driven through humid hours like orchids in a cooler, and others all azalea, wild pink shrubs that trumpeted in hot places, flagrant and profuse. Night came on so strong there, the smear of color and funereal perfume, every bloom corpulent on flood and rain. My friend and I walked the Quarter eating butter pastry and oysters. Six feet tall, she glowed against the courtyard—Venus, a marble goddess, who tasted the world's saliva as if it were champagne. Sax men poured tunes like hot cane just to make my friend laugh. When Venus danced, flowers opened. Freaks spun round her like multicolored ribbons. As if she groomed her handsome children, my friend embraced men with faces shaped like figs. She kept a pond for beasts behind a black iron fence, behind the Quarter on Lesseps Street, and a gravestone in the grass. Near dawn I slept on her guest bed, sweating against red satin, while a silver fan clacked overhead. Sun cut through leaded windows, spun the air to hot glass. Black coffee with thick cream, huge strawberries in a mahogany dining room. We hid from the heat and talked of dying— the flickering boats our fathers rode to the spirit world, the little hulls of morphine. As the air began to wave and drip, we walked the streets again, both dressed in white gauze with crisp straw hats, then wispy, drooping damp. We headed for her levee shack, three lilting rooms of bird nests. Water, the dissolving river, lapped the back porch, the pilings. *Tell me about a lover,* she'd say, causing a lip of wine to sing under her index finger. We never touched, but in the tuberous wave of our voices, we drifted for days. As I drove north one dark, past St. Charles and into the bayou, a rainstorm changed the livid horizon to brown, then bruise. How sweet azaleas at the beginning, breathing in the swamps, breathing in the streets, their fuschia bodies covering our feet. How brief our beauty in sugared heat—our dresses lifted and fell those hours between the wicker and dying rafters like opulent clouds of steam.

Worms

Some days he'd rub two pegs together
until they made a greasy hum
like rain, the sound of moles
gnawing the dirt's grain, the song
soils sing before a quake,
and the red bodies would hang
above the ground in a kind of confusion
or ecstasy. They would writhe.

The farmer showed me
the way worms made love
in concrete, coffin-shaped beds
on mattresses of moss and peat, slipping
under the rubber collars of each other,
joyous, shy, nervous, taking turns.
Androgynous worms, their pale larva
rising like dew on black earth.

He told me about the sweet spot
in the warm dirt where he found
the wild ones, night crawlers
a foot long. How he worked
day and night—plastic sky
dripping on his neck—preached
on Sundays, sixteen years old,
reeking of worm sweat.

We drove around his slow
Louisiana Baptist town, the square
garlanded with green metallic boughs,
red Noels, though it was October.
There was one movie house.
The Bijou of course. First floor—
expensive, gummy, for whites only.
Blacks sat in the rafters for a quarter.

Filmy bayous surrounded
blank brown cotton fields,
fluttered with white heron.
Once a black man walked

by a white girl and she ran.
He never said hello. The citizens
dragged him from prison,
burned the man alive.

But that's an old story.
This one's new—a black boy
sat in that same prison five years,
innocent too, and when the town freed him
he headed for a Victorian house
he'd watched each night like television—
the illuminated window
of an eighty-year-old couple—

he knifed them both, raped the woman,
what felons become legend to.
If you tend worms your whole life,
dig their beds, stir the eggs,
sort the dark segmented bodies,
you'll lose the pattern of your own
flesh. The whorls of your fingers
will vanish. A worm can eat anything—

two by four, dog, human.
I know this world, said the farmer,
I've listened to worms my whole life
stirring in slime. I know where
we come from, and despite all our slick
designs, I know where we return.
This town's passed more than once
through the slippery tunnels of worms.

Card Game Blind River

I was not afraid of the alligator gar exploding round the boat,
the ghostly songs of nutria, the scraping palmetto, nor tales of hunters
frozen in their keels, waves folded over them like blankets.

I felt like dancing. Grass dead. Pond scum frozen. Ice made me happy.
The natives liked to scare me. Come spring, they'd say, snakes'll twist
around your paddle like spaghetti, drop out of branches

right into your boat. One guy shot a hole in his *pirogue*—
stump snake, big as an arm, aggressive.
Later we lit a fire in camp, the flare of whiskey,

of friends' breath. We played a card game, *Pedro*—
five high, ace low. My partner a *connai*,
which meant he could read my mind. I was losing.

Light drumming began on the ceiling, like shells boiling in a pot,
fingernails on a tabletop, high heels tapping, the attic smoked
and bodies wove through each other. We could not see them,

but dreaming nests of rattlesnakes were coming to life. *Ah, M'sieu Serpent*
said my partner. Surely he could hear the high *e* of my mind.
It sang like a car alarm, though I continued slapping down my hand. Bluffing.

Hadn't I learned hurricane—leeches on the porch, window glass
melting, trees grunting, moss standing straight up.
These people were afraid of nothing—iron crosses, gargoyles,

trumpets of flame—that's how they prayed.
Wouldn't you be terrified. What was this game.
Damnit to hell. Was I the only human.

A Warrior's Tale

We sat under a rotunda, so the smallest sound reverberated, came back historic. Richard told a story about hiking alone in the woods of northern California, how he found the decomposing body of a young woman. She was still alive. There were maggots crawling in her hands. She'd been raped, pushed over a cliff, and she had crawled back up with broken bones, to even ground, to be found or left to die. Richard told this story in front of Rachel. It must have been a kind of warrior's tale. A young man had broken into Rachel's apartment in the French Quarter. She moved back into the same apartment after the attack. Everyone thought her brave. The man had raped her, then stabbed her in the chest with her own butcher knife—she almost died of perforated lungs—and as he stabbed, he asked her, *will you be my sweetheart?* and she begged, *please call an ambulance.* Rachel broke down when she heard Richard's story, but she broke down in another room so that the men could not see her.

The Stray Sod

A place charmed by faeries where you enter
knowing everything and then are lost.

Even though you started on a small errand,
even though it was nothing, like waxing
a refrigerator door or weeding the detroit reds,
and you knew the path, remember
how easily the granite fit your arch,
how the timothy parted at your knees,
and you heard the charmed scale
of a flauty thrush, then the smell
of a vagrant riverbed, the leaning
ironwood fence threaded with yellow roses,
the abandoned circle of chairs?
You passed the place where robins
cemented a nest each year and grew babies
the size of throw pillows. You walked
the lily moon and the blanketflower,
past prize offers no one could refuse,
till you entered a spinning barrel,
and you began to burn. You can turn
your coat now, you can go in disguise,
but you will recognize nothing, not one face
smeared against the blind forest, not one word.
The gate is gone and the path
erased behind you. Goodness is deception.
Flesh—deception in the churning oaks.
Remember the fun house, the dark-wooded
chutes, all those mouths laughing
at your blistered limbs out of control?
The world allows no virgin. Not for long.
If you're happy, you're young.
You'll catch on. Strike two fingers.
See if you can find a pulse.

Taboo

Like a marriage. Like a nation. Like a haunting, this story tells me. Often from the stranger's view. How he stood over me while I slept. My lover and I must have looked like a pair of white summer shoes—sweaty, exhausted. I live in a renovated shotgun. Cypress floors, cut-glass windows. We keep our doors locked here, windows curtained. Perfumed skin hidden under perfumed linen. The stranger sat in my living room a long time. Smoked a cigarette. Crossed his legs, watched the cat lick her back legs, the space between each claw. Some people say I shouldn't have let him get away. He was not respectful to your home. Not respectful to your property. But he did not harm me, and he was not the first to enter a space defined taboo. Every job I ever took was to get close to someone who had been separated from me. I slept inside a nunnery. I became an exchange teacher for an all-black college. The Chairman told me he knew a white professor who carried an inflatable raft in his van, in case of a riot, he would float the Mississippi out of harm's way. The students in my night class said I should stop apologizing for history, *we know your daddy didn't keep slaves.* But I never understood my role in history, so when that man stood over the bed, I did not really see him, and I did not want to know what his color might be. Maybe I should say person, but he smelled like a man, and his movements were awkward—after a lifetime of picking up clothes, folding sheets, a woman would move more quietly through another woman's bedroom. The first time I heard him, he was a few feet from my head. My parents shifted in their silver frame. And then the rocker. A sound no louder than a moth bumping a lamp shade. My lover snored beside me. We'd been drinking vodka, and the room must have smelled vinegary. I knew if I moved, I would jeopardize my lover's life, the stranger's, mine, and for what, it was not a robbery the stranger was committing, it was a touching. How many times had my eye opened a lace curtain to circle a neighbor's rooms. When the deadbolt slid, my lover sat up, groaned, lay down again. I stepped barefoot onto the front stoop. Concrete rose cool against my instep. Perhaps this story repeats itself because the bodies need to be told back to life. I felt like a piece of property curled inanimate between those two men. The law shaped our disposition. A kind of resource management made us taboo. I knotted a robe about my waist and waited. The neighborhood was disturbed now—Great Danes, Dobermans crackling over grape leaves. I wanted the stranger to talk to me. I leaned against the railing and waited. A Cyclone fence separated the houses, and I guessed he stood on the other side. *I can see you,* I said, though nothing but spider lilies were visible, long lobed, shivering, their suffocating perfume. I knew he smelled them too. *I can see you.* Each night of their blooming they shine ultraviolet, insinuate themselves into our dreams. There are giant moths that hover above them. It's a life's work. To sip and gather. To hover. Above these murky waters.

He Paints the Kingdom of Decay: His Goddess Escapes

Thirty-one days of October the opalescent monsoons
roll over like gray eggs, viscous, pooling earth to clay,
filling grass with oily skinks and pink-mouthed alligators.

I lie in bed near noon and do not rise
but turn over and over in sweaty sheets
behind the bamboo curtains.

Outside the window a loquat fattens, and on its branches
a mockingbird creaks and clinks *rain, rain,*
his warble—the lip-blown crystal of a chandelier.

Thirty-one days of rain, like making love again,
again with no release. This is no season,
mushed together and sticky as gumbo.

The mourning doves try to form themselves
from dun-colored leaves, and I, from a pattern
of mire and bruise, recall only two visions.

In one, a painter's studio drips with women
bathing in green. Circe hangs in each room,
naked, choked with vegetation.

Rubens might have painted her blue
among the porcine suitors, lumpy
and sweet as sherbet, let the waterlilies

bloom yellow. She could have floated
the Bogue Falaya with purple muscadine
and fleshy bougainvillea.

But the swamp artist, sick of the rain, the clammy
garret of his brain, suffocates his goddess,
lets her rot in sugar cane and soft mud.

For days I amble about in a body, dilapidated
as a caged animal, until I stop to rest under
a ligustrum canopy and watch Circe herself

come splashing through the parking lot,
top down on her red convertible,
unplaited, razor-cut hair flapping.

Another season I might have noted
her flashy clothes, underbitten chin,
the irritating habit she has of licking

her knuckles, but I welcome her now
in every muscle, as if—bright escapee racing
diffused sun—she has the charm to soothe the rain,

to turn us human again. Such is beauty:
blood stopper, burn healer, enchanter of warts.
As she cuts the corner close to my sandals, close

to my red painted toes, her waxy car brushes against me.
Afterwards, there is a perfume of cucumbers. Saxophones
sigh from her radio to the saturated leaves.

Rags

The piebald dog, the scalded shreds
of a dream, the moment when the valley
sleeps, when it's only heart
and the cardinal singing—red ripe rags.

I like the way the single white hairs
shine in my head and the lids
over my eyes sag. When I come home
from work at night, I strip.

I drink rum and listen to stumbling
plots on television. I drink
until my brain slides, until the suit
melts, washes from my body

and I am naked, dark and light
as a stilt bird with brown eyes,
slick crown and laugh lines.
Oh we each have our vanity—

the amethyst silk, the hard-polished agate,
pearls from an oyster's craw,
and we covet most the things well broken
by the body: one split-pawed glove;

the sculpture in a friend's small room,
not the one she carved from marble,
but flawed alabaster. Hauled from the Pyrenees,
soft and rough, gouged like creamy butter,

the head, cradled in a smooth skull,
looks like a girl who wants to break loose
from her own body by crawling
through a ragged face.

In the Jittering World

I carry a chameleon in a glass as if he were wild game.
I herd him from the oak floor
                              where he mimics the grain
toward the living room
                              to bathe in a saucer of brown water
under the ficus tree. He climbs the plum sofa and lies
under my reading lamp. Slowly he warms himself.
Slowly we warm together—oh the fine intellect of winter.
No antelope would sit so still
                              content to glow against fuschia pillows
blinking from rouge to green with no nervous movement,
                              no perceptible throb in his throat.

In a world jittering with possibility,
                              how did I come to this sour basement
in a Southern city to grade rhetoric,
                              water dripping all day down drainpipes,
and at night for recreation,
to nurse a lizard? I love his sticky toe pads,
the way he rests
                              between death and life, leaf-veined, reflective.
Carefully he picks across the blue carpet, as if
it were a globe laid flat.
                              Perhaps we both are lost in our landscape,
woman and chameleon always changing to save our skin.

I toss down a piece of butter lettuce which rocks on the carpet
like a pallid sail.
                              Might he be melancholy?
Can iguanas experience
                              the macabre, uncanny?
I make what offering I can. I leave on the incandescent lamp
when I go to bed, for this fawn-spotted scholar,
                              this saturnine antelope
settling against the sofa cushions, the only beacons
flicking in a cool dendritic body—his bulging eyes
                              aquatic, otherworldly
                              slow like mine.

Possessions

Veronika said when her father died, the mother moved from their family home in Israel. The mother could not bear to live with the family possessions, and the children did not want to sell them. A twenty-seven-year-old man rented the house. When she became lonely, Veronika's mother visited the young man. She sat among the samovars and enameled spice boxes, the cups with gold edges. She inhaled smoke that permeated the carpets—wood and kerosene, incense, candles. The renter, a mathematician, brought her small hard butter cookies shaped like zeros with sesame seeds on the surface, and she dipped them in her tea. In time she confused him with her own family. He took on their smell. The mother's children were in a country so far away, she could not imagine them. Her daughter, Veronika, wrote that she lived beside a swamp in Louisiana. Veronika, a fine medievalist, had been hired by a Southern university to teach remedial students in a basement that flooded each afternoon. Like workers who give their lives over to the machine and never talk about their sadness or resignation, Veronika and I worked side by side in that basement for years. Now we were both leaving, and Veronika was telling me this story. We stood in a parking lot after midnight. As though she kept the door of her own house closed, she cracked it for a moment so I could see inside to its mysterious tapestry. For years, Veronika said, her mother wrote that she visited the family house and the young mathematician who served her zeroes with black tea. When she died, Veronika's brother flew to Israel to visit the mother's grave, to sell the house and divide its possessions. He discovered the family estate empty. Completely empty. The stone house echoed. It had no smell. The mathematician had sold everything, a piece at a time, to the Arabic and Jewish flea markets. A year later the police located the mathematician, doing what mathematicians often do, occupying himself with calculations in a bare room. During the trial, the mathematician hanged himself. Later, in a junk shop, the brother found a photograph of Veronika. Later still, the entire family album. And that was all.

The Bureau of Unclaimed Property

The program's two-person staff is too small to do much searching.

~

An elderly woman dies without telling anyone about a long-forgotten savings.

~

On her wall, the framed dress of a dead sister, cross-stitched
hair flowers, last wisps cut from her auburn head.
Charity needled to the wall.

~

The state keeps trying to help people lay claim to property.

~

A jewel box with photographs of wrecked vehicles.

~

Paper weights and smooth bone bullets.

~

You broke my heart, *cher.*

~

You stayed so good Aimee.

~

To claim property a person must prove she is legal.

~

In six layers of net petticoats, red, off-the-shoulder dress, rouged cheeks,
she carries two trophies, one for *Miss Eight-Year-Old Acadienne,*
the other for *Miss Personality.*

~

The office is filling a locked file cabinet with bits and pieces of people's lives.

~

From the radio:
I just want to talk to somebody. I mean there's Joanie, but I don't want to be bothering my friends. I just got to ta
Get away from myself. I mean. I know I can go out, look around, but sometimes you just want
to get your mind off it, you know.

~

Houses rushing downriver
fish swimming
through each room
human faces
at the window.

~

Alligators suspended like pickles in a murky salt solution.

~

Gowns hanging from white branches.
Belles selling frocks beside putty-colored mansions.
Men running over lawns at dusk, their breasts shaking.

~

Someone forgets about putting them into
a safe deposit box

~

Last month's list contained thousands of names.

~

We eat slowly for hours, drink champagne. Elegant sauces in a green room
perfect clarets, perfect rice. The chef in impeccable whites
shoves us past a glazed piano.

~

bandoned property held by the state in hopes one day the rightful owner or heir will come forward.

~

I stand precise beside opulent roses,
my father's palms frightened into fists, his lips curved downward.
The embalming fluid has turned him an unnatural shade of blue.

~

At dusk an old man on his porch tuning a fiddle.

~

A gathering of church people, misshapen, goiter-eyed, swallow sea dogs
with Dr Pepper. One takes an order to a black man
who waits in the corner of their van.

~

A list of apparent owners of property.

~

Car lights shining under water.

~

A bag with a miniature padlock.

~

A brooch, a cuff link and a tiny gray thimble.

~

Forever
they're going to be held
in the names of the owners and their heirs.
Some of the items have obvious worth,
others have value known
only to the dead.

Maximum Security

So I was sticking
to my nylon teddy, unraveling
the lace—pink
like crepe myrtle, pink
like raspberry sorbet,

when the lady on the radio
said a Green Beret escaped
Angola Maximum Security,
walked straight into a cornfield.
First his tracks disappeared,

then bloodhounds lost his scent.
If you were born to a gooey
bayou, two faithless fathers,
a silent mother, sleazy clouds
overhead for pillows,

you'd celebrate too. I dream
of North, a place cool enough
to think. My friend James says
he'd take me to the Rockies,
but mountains give him nosebleeds.

Don't get me wrong, I like my neighbors—
the way Mrs. Walker swings all day,
showing off her panties. Mostly I feel
as though I'm riding on an airplane,
air conditioner running,

piped-in Pachelbel. Palmetto bugs
storm the windows as if I ran
a bright casino. German roaches
in tight brown suits. On Alcatraz
guards locked the worst offenders

closest to the bay, so they could smell
chocolate melting in the factory.
Our mayor is unhappy. *That soldier's*

deadly dangerous, he says.
He's planted himself

a few feet underground
like a goddamned Neanderthal.
Call off the dogs. Bring in the plows.
And who doesn't pray
for the deadly dangerous.

Bedtime when the mosquito sprayer
sleeps, I crack my window, scan
the puddly horizon for that Green Beret,
spy the neon grass. I wear a split chemise.
I listen for his breathing.

In Case of Rapture This Taxi Will Explode

Would you ride with a man who advertised
the ecstatic. Would you expect him
dressed in a pressed shirt, sandals.
Would you have a destination. He takes me
by surprise. *My lady,* he says.
His quiet hands. He reads the Bible.
Shyness can be graphed you know—
the distance one stands from another human.
Shyness is a constellation. Warlike societies
require manly perfection, a cloak for violence,
a hero who is different from mine.
After the coup, the city was quiet at night
except for gunfire and the birds.
Skin-colored lizards eating mosquitoes.
Too soon our ride was over. Nothing now
but a small cluster of tulips blooming
like heavy-headed committee members
in my rented rooms, tossing off petals
pink and white, like too many speeches
to the shining glass table. In the icebox,
one tropical beer, a succulent lime.
Cooling. With what sharp
pleasure I would welcome
company into my life.

Burying the Carnival

*Oh sweet world soaked like bread
in sweet milk for the terrible toothless God.*
YEHUDA AMICHI

Fat Tuesday the parade route turned
on Canal Street, passed through spitting
pink flambeaux. Toothless kings in plumed hats
threw backscratchers, plastic grenades.
Knights in leopardskin and blackface
flashed their signs. *Show your tits.*
Knives and coconuts a special prize.

I can't breathe, screamed an old man,
his fist landing against my cheek.
Lemme outta here. Chicken skin pavement
greased our stampede. Locked in the center,
spinning like a turnstile, I thought I would surely die,
Carnival riding gaily by, bright smears of blood,
doubloons flying and purple beads.

Breathe, I said to my body
as the crowd panicked through
the streets, *breathe,* fifteen minutes
my feet touched nothing.
I had always been wild, willing
to be seized by divinity, but silently
and alone. I feared the soul

abandoned me, though it complained
inside my skull like wasps
against a ceiling, it would be years
before I would enter a crowd,
stand in line, ride an airplane,
years before I would let
the world close again.

~

And then comes a holiday just as the wasps are waking, nights fill with
people, a parade of friends, but painted up, changed. A pig fed all win-
ter by hand is chased through the streets. Nothing in his brain pre-
pares him for this. His cry is terrible. Drunken revelers rub each other,

politicians, the heir to the mustard and pickle fortune. Midnight the phone rings, a Northern voice calls my name, *this is Larry, I am reading* The Cherry Orchard, *guess where I have my hands.* I do not know the voice, cannot see his face, the rest of civilization holds up its mask to laugh at me.

~

Because Carnival is a pageant.

Because people float slowly Saturday nights through the mall,
      like fish in a tank, their mouths moving, stopping at one glass,
            then another. They skip on a wave of nervous laughter,
                a high sweet noise in their throats.

Because civilization can conceal our true nature.

Because the boy hangs on his mother's shoulders, he could be dancing,
      his face a grimace, a perfectly round hole on his spine,
            dark maroon against a red baseball jacket.

Because Carnival is Jesus, a general or a sinner.

Because we had an aquarium with one blue bass, two crawfish,
      a large mud turtle, the crawfish held the bass in their pinchers, fed
            its flesh into their mouths, the lips of the bass spoke slowly,
                then the turtle ate the crawfish, shells and all.

Because the turtle lives forever, even headless refuses to die.

Because Carnival is crucified, beheaded, drowned, burned, shot,
      or just buried alive. Because Carnival is an effigy.
            Because the effigy wears enormous boots and a tin
                helmet. His gestures are controlled by strings.

Because a small citizen rides under His mercy seat to pull the strings.

Because the crowd remains sweaty years later, bags crashing
      down chutes, women spinning in costumes,
            men churning shirtless torsos.

Because Carnival is given brandy or a speech and He comes back to life.

Because people clothed as beasts drag beasts from the bayou—
        possum, rat, nutria, armadillo, little spine bones
                in the gumbo, crawfish, coon.

Because the four-hundred-pound king snores on his float
        of palmetto and animal bodies.

Because the prince dances with the queen who totters on her pumps,
        leading her by mammoth hips, steering her enormous breasts
                until she abandons him for a toothless skeleton of a man.

Because Carnival is a fugitive stage of rapture.

Because after all, the dipping yachts look gay,
        until we see the blue heads,
                the watery faces watching through the trees.

Sweat

Charles Olson's "I, Maximus/ a metal hot from boiling water" might have been the lyric sung on the backlot of the body shop where I grew up—paint fumes, grease pans, sparks flying—surrounded by Serbs, Germans, Hungarians returned from the Second World War, men who saw themselves, no matter how confusing, in direct lineage from the gods. Oh there were the fallen—Dale, for instance, who lived on a houseboat in the middle of a cornfield, drove an ancient Cadillac convertible, and stole women's girdles from clotheslines—but mostly these were supermen. I studied their calendars of women with bombshell breasts and skirts always given to the wind, and when I could get my hands on them, I read their nude sunbathing magazines. These were men unlike those I would meet in college, love or marry, but I studied them as we ate at my grandmother's table, the sounds they made so different from mine.

I grew up on an acre between Dixie Highway and the Illinois Central tracks where trains raced hourly through fields of wild asparagus. In the dream space between two lines of speeding technology was a grape arbor; a fish pond; a house full of women sunk to their elbows in bread dough; fields of geese, goats, sugar pear trees; the graves of bloody cars and grass grown crystalline through cracked windshields. I baked with the aunts and fished silently with the uncles and felt at home on the periphery of both worlds surrounded by action and accompanying sound. My grandfather whittled, sanded, banged, and snored. My grandmother—on a tonic of garlic and wine—fried, kneaded, waltzed. Together each day they spoke raucous Platt und Hochdeutsch. *I did not participate in their conversation, nor the bodymen's jokes, the spray painting, the bumping and welding, the straightening of steel, though those too are dialects I know.*

And when I went off to college I lied. I denied that I had won blue ribbons for butterscotch bars and tight little stitches in skirts, because that was female, and I denied I'd grown up in a body shop, because that was laughable, lower class, and not female. So began a dance, of learning then denying experience. Not exactly the way to build intelligence, though silence sharpens the senses, creates an oily, pungent memory.

Dancing the Tarentella at the County Farm

Our teachers prepared us years ahead
so that when I laze in bed past noon
twenty years later, ignoring my late father's
imperative-voice command—
get up and blow the stink off—
the poorhouse floats back to me
through its allée of hardwood trees.
It resembles a Georgian estate
surrounded by plate-flat farmland
and rumor that the basement
housed a torture chamber.
Our dogpatch class of nine-year-olds
grows suddenly grave as we approach.
Inside brick walls and flowered wallpaper
inmates have just finished lunch,
something like dried oatmeal
pasted to their trays, something difficult
to scrape away. Their faces have that same texture.
Our caretakers resemble each other—
same desire for order, same steel-arched shoes.
Each year they march us to the community room
to share each other's shame. My invitation—
to dance for the lady in a wheelchair, to display
long muscular legs. *You're all she has,* says the teacher
as she straightens my homemade costume.
But I am third grade. A nothing. I think
I'll never escape. Stronger than a father's voice,
the whisper of my teacher. *Bow deeply
from stage left,* her breath fused with the face
of the paralyzed woman, *and when the music begins
get out there fast.* I spin, I split, I do back flips.
I become St. Vitus again. I dance the spider bite
as hard as I can. See, I smile. Good girl.
My body becomes a wet rag. I wring it tighter and tighter.
Like a dervish. Like a top. It wants to fall over.
It wants to give up. If love were water
not a drop would be left.

Artie

Among the claw-foot sofas, under the looming
mahogany of my grandparents' living room,
the hoodlum and I played with flames—

while Grandmother slept under chicken feathers
and Grandfather snored in his separate bedroom
above my head. *Strop, strop*

Grandpa's razor would bite its black strap.
His bumping hammer could flatten fenders.
Thank god he was deaf and drunk.

Smart ass punk, that's what people called Artie,
weasel trash, this gypsy who rubbed against me
grating his pink lips into my braces.

Mrs. Molenda's grandson came from the West Side
to clean her pigeon cages, and he became the rebel boy
of Dixie Highway for girls whose daddies owned

the gas station, the Dairy Queen, the bait and tackle.
Artie had the whitest teeth and his dark Hungarian skin sheened
where I reached to stroke behind his waist and earlobes.

I was fourteen and months later found myself on hands and knees
scrubbing linoleum for the first time above a tavern on the West Side,
hanging limp café curtains with hopeful rickrack snowballs,

for my friend Laurie, a shy, cracked-tooth towhead
who had the body of a boy, and for Artie and their baby—
who'd curl on their beaten mohair sofa cooing just like us.

The Red Dress

Cousin Char and I are doing the *Splendor in the Grass* thing, where the lover comes back to town to view her old flame caught in merciless circumstances. My childhood sweetheart pumps gas these days, but that's a career change. He spent time in prison. He was a pimp. My cousin Char is an interpretive dancer who lives in a trailer on Newport Beach. She cultivates a bohemian life. She sells dolls at swap meets. It is summer and we have flown to the Midwest to stalk her old dance partner— Nikos, the Greek boy who tapped like Sammy Davis. His father made him work in the family fruit market, permitted him to dance only for Greek Orthodox events. Char says the Greek elders paired her with Nikos on stage as if they were a mythical romance everyone loved, but kept apart—Romeo and that white girl. I have been inventing Nikos' life for the last twenty-five years. I have been inventing all our lives, how one day we would return spectacular and immune to our high-school gymnasium. But first, Nikos would escape his job in the Acropolis Market, move to New York, kick like a Rockette, become indescribably gay. We would see him featured on the Tonys. Char says not exactly. When she last spoke with Nikos, he had joined a cult, dressed in orange robes, traveled to India. Char's brother, who sells hearing aids, says Nikos did come back to the Midwest a few years before he died. He had hair down to his waist and had lost his front teeth. He worked in the family fruit market. Char and I are standing in front of the Acropolis Market. There is a special on fruit baskets. Twenty-five years there has been a special on fruit baskets. In Nikos' obituary, the family declined to mention that Nikos was a dancer, that he danced one night for the longest running musical on Broadway. Char and I are doing the girl thing—refusing to let old boyfriends rest, trying to understand them, even in death. When Nikos came home to die, he asked the stately wife of his childhood friend to be a pallbearer and to wear a red dress when she carried his coffin. Half his life Nikos had performed under the gold dome of the Orthodox church. He wore the white chemise of Greek chieftains. He danced the labyrinth, the dance of spoons. Half his life he wanted to wear the red dress. We savor this detail, as though it will make life comprehensible. I imagine the dress cut high and on the bias, so that it slithers down his torso before it flares. From the sidewalk we peer through the plate glass of the Acropolis at a young boy who wraps baskets with yellow cellophane. By the far-off look in his eyes, we know he is Nikos' nephew. Perhaps he too will become a star. Char and I agree, as he ribbons red bananas from the rainforests of Dominica, blood oranges from Mexico, this boy makes our blood tingle.

Sweat

Friday night I entered a dark corridor
rode to the upper floors with men who filled
the stainless elevator with their smell.

Did you ever make a crystal garden, pour salt
into water, keep pouring until nothing more dissolved?
A landscape will bloom in that saturation.

My daddy's body shop floats to the surface
like a submarine. Men with nibblers and tin snips
buffing skins, sanding curves under clamp lights.

I grew up curled in the window of a 300 SL
Gullwing, while men glided on their backs
through oily rainbows below me.

They torqued lugnuts, flipped fag ends
into gravel. Our torch song
had one refrain—*oh the pain of loving you.*

Friday nights they'd line the shop sink, naked
to the waist, scour down with Ajax, spray water
across their necks and up into their armpits.

Babies have been conceived on sweat alone—
the buttery scent of a woman's breast,
the cumin of a man. From the briny odor

of black lunch boxes—cold cuts, pickles,
waxed paper—my girl flesh grows.
From the raunchy fume of strangers.

The Assembly Line

If you saw Mercedes-Benz flying
from the loading dock, warehouse rafters in flames,
you might think *Luftwaffe*—Hitler's Madonna Lilies,
eighteen coats of sleek ivory enameled over steel—

might not see the *oompahs* who made the limousines,
men grown thick from *Schuhmacher,* sausage stitched
with leather thread into a pig's belly, Freedom Fighters
who chamoised bumpers with their underwear, Hunkies

like Pete Kudla who dusted each chassis with a sable hair brush,
taped, blasted till layers of paint collapsed his lungs. After he died,
his wife Dorothy baked our thousand Christmas *keeflies*
in her teardrop trailer—apricot, walnut, poppyseed.

If you saw Mercedes flying, you'd remember the heroes
who drove lockjawed through black smoke, but might not see
their families—my mother, the bookkeeper, who looked
like Rita Hayworth, who tallied columns in the summer kitchen

by the sink where we butchered chickens,
or my grandmother, who fattened us all from soup vats,
then waltzed away afternoons in the Black Forest
of her living room in a garlic-smelling housedress.

We prayed hard for those Mercedes, and after flames
that filled the streets with wrinkled charred limousines,
we crossed Western Avenue to the Hunky Dory Café
where we ate *piroshki,* danced the heel-toe polka,

raised steins with my father, Karl Weis,
his partner George Grochowski, bodymen grown
like gods before our eyes from a grandmother's
diet of songbirds and lard. And who was I—

thin as a string, daughter of the best bump and ding
in the whole United States, as I crouched behind
the pop machine in the body shop, memorizing
poses from girlie magazines?

Hats

Auntie lies in the rest home with a feeding tube and a bedpan, she weighs nothing, she fidgets and shakes, and all I can see are her knotted hands and the carbon facets of her eyes, she was famous for her pies and her kindness to neighbors, but if it is true that every hat exhibits a drama the psyche wishes it could perform, what was my aunt saying all the years of my childhood when she squeezed into cars with those too tall hats, those pineapples and colored cockades, my aunt who told me I should travel slowly or I would see too much before I died, wore spires and steeples, tulled toques. The velvet inkpots of Schiaparelli, the mousseline de soie of Lilly Daché have disappeared into the world, leaving behind one flesh-colored box, *Worth* stenciled on the top, a coral velvet cloche inside with matching veil and drawstring bag, and what am I to make of these Dolores del Rio size 4 black satin wedgies with constellations of spangles on the bridge. Before she climbed into the white boat of the nursing home and sailed away—talking every day to family in heaven, calling them through the sprinkling system—my aunt said she was pushing her cart through the grocery when she saw young girls at the end of an aisle pointing at her, her dowager's hump, her familial tremors. Auntie, who claimed that ninety pounds was her fighting weight, carried her head high, hooded, turbaned, jeweled, her neck straight under pounds of roots and vegetables that shimmied when she walked. Surely this is not the place of women in our world, that when we are old and curled like crustaceans, young girls will laugh at us, point their fingers, run as fast as they can in the opposite direction.

The Limits of Beauty

When I am sad I buff and shine,
drive the scenic route, eat Swiss chocolates
the size of golf balls, toss down rum shooters,
pick the resurrection lilies, place them
in an amber vase. Last summer a ghost
rolled over while I scythed knapweed in a field,
Ave Maria blasting from the radio,
and the face of my old friend floated before me.
Okay, I said, tell me what I need to know
about this world. *Love beauty,* she said.
She died young, tortured near the end.
Weeks before, we'd talked of life. Both agreed
we knew nothing. But that night when the dogs
woke me, their hackles perpendicular,
her chiffon robe drifted over my body.
Its soft hem startled me. Her mother buried her
in calico, as if she were going to a dance.
Do astral bodies change to evening clothes?
No matter what I know, the sky goes on spinning
its blue and white ballet, toe heel, toe heel, grand jeté.
With each turn the syllables *alone alone alone.*
I attend the theater. A man reads about skin diving
off a Caribbean island—the aroma of lemon grass,
of *fleur d'amour.* His language makes him feverish.
He locks a gaze on me. I pull out my eyebrows
distractedly one black hair at time, study them
as they grow on the white program.
He finishes his poem about the miraculous
cathedrals of neon fish. I yawn deeply.
The dark bristles of my body just fly away.

Because the Body Is Not a Weapon

In this town of date palms
and expensive pastry
everyone wears pastels.
Everyone owns a sports car
and speeds. I leap with blondes
in a gymnasium of steely leotards.
No one speaks to me.
No one catches my eye.
I eat ill-conceived
Mexican takeout—
pasty beans with
chopped beef.
In my dreams
all the creeps of my life
call me. I swear the only person
who spoke last week
had three-inch toenails
curled over his sandals.
Oh yes, and at the grocery
a little girl in coveralls
studies me when I smile.
You're not my mother,
she kicks her thick legs
through the cart rails.
You're   not   my   mother.
Still I pass lightly
as a dust diamond
through my pink sea cottage.
And how should I take this omen:
stalled in traffic, a van of boys
barks at me. Twelve years old,
they lick the windows.
They moon their half-formed buttocks.
They wiggle their shell-like genitals.
Do I laugh?
Have I become a foreign country?

Zulu Time

Only my cousin with high blood pressure traveled widely. He was certain he did not have long to live, so he took up flying. He refused to marry or have children. Not because he was trying to escape responsibility, as he pointed out, the whole world is on Zulu Time, which used to be called Mean Time. Even airspace 18,000 feet over your head is controlled, though from a great altitude, the earth appears to stand still. He flew around the world. He visited the grave of Eva Perón. Near her crypt there was a black box on a post. The box had windows on three sides. My cousin put his hand inside. When he returned home, he brought a turquoise hat for his girlfriend he had purchased in Argentina. She walked outside to let the sunshine filter through the straw hat. It was there she saw something strange—an object quivering like a leaf of paper. *What did you put on your shoes?* She looked very festive with her red lips and striped hat. *Did you put something on your shoes?* My cousin crossed the patio. There was indeed something dark flexing on the toe of his shoe. The same pair he'd worn at the grave site of Eva Perón. Quietly he slid the screendoor open, went to the kitchen and returned with a glass jar. He held the jar over the toe. It was a bat. He knew that he had brought it all the way from Argentina in his suitcase, that it had come from the black box beside the grave of Eva Perón. He remembered that a bat might have rabies. That in China a bat was symbolic of happiness and long life. He is a kind man who does not like to hold another captive. Still most nights he wakes, sneaks downstairs to look at the bat. What if a bat can live forever sealed off with almost no air. He never thought himself a superstitious man, but what if this is no bat at all that has entered his life. He shakes the jar. Does it only appear to be drying up, to be getting smaller.

Salvation Army

Pennsylvania Dutch, my family taught me
the humility of secondhand. Taken up,
mended, trued, nothing can be thrown away.

Dining table stripped and sanded, curly maple
Hoosier cabinet, stringless dulcimer. Mission sofa hauled
from a deserted cabin where the rancher died of tuberculosis.

Signature quilts with cigarette burns, any piece of muslin
needled by a woman's hand. But I long to live
plain—a Shaker spinning in a bare room.

Anchorites had themselves entombed alive
so they might concentrate on God.
Not even flaming buttresses could move them.

I circle the Salvation Army. Display windows
feature last month's holidays—Valentine bends over
a wicker table, her red acetate kimono open.

Wig cocked at forty-five degrees, she serves
Saint Patrick tea. A man who resembles
Saint Jerome leans against the cinderblock

eyeing me, from my green lambswool muffler
to my Red Wings. I eye him back. Same age.
Same size. From the hollow cheeks I'd guess

it's not his first time on the mend. *Hi gorgeous,*
he says. I open the lid to my donation. He fingers
the suits and slippers of my dead uncles,

their Zippos and feed caps. How light I feel as he
lifts my family from me. If I were Aztec
I'd bring them back one day each year,

roll their beds to the grave hung with black lace,
pay two sad men to play accordian, make an offering
of marigolds, tamales. Ghosts love aroma.

But my dead uncles—how they carry on.
Happy to be away from home, they jump
this toothless stranger, wave their porkpie hats.

He drags them to his favorite tavern. They swear
they've gone to heaven as they sink into his smokey booth,
his cardgame, his moon-shaped platter of brains and eggs.

Feeding the Babies

In her eightieth year, my mother cries for a baby, she lifts her hands to the sky, does the baby dance, and out of sheer loneliness a baby is born. After all, didn't God make humans from a need for companions. *Don't be jealous,* my mother says when I shake a rattle in the newborn's face. It is salty and wiggles like a grunion. My mother takes the baby to her bed, her giant Italian provincial made of pecan wood. She bathes it in her orchid-papered bathroom. She cradles the baby in her arms and they watch *Oprah* together, *Geraldo, cluck cluck* she says, *the world is a scary place,* she takes a sip of her Old Fashioned and breathes over the baby. She names the baby Candy and drives it to Family Gardens for chicken on Sunday, Polish sausage buffets on Saturday at the Skillet. My mother feeds her baby right there at the table. It sits on a little throne. Her friends grow jealous of this ancient widow who tends a newborn that is dewy as a fuschia bloom. Even when it howls and throws potatoes. And what do I learn of maternal instinct by watching my mother. Mostly I observe how partnering becomes more felicitous and improbable with age. Her friends wrap their chicken wings, their bratwurst and garlic bread in paper napkins, stick them in patent leather pocketbooks to carry out to the parking lot where tiny Cockapoos curl in the back windows of Oldsmobiles, sunning. Newly bathed, the dogs are wrapped in pastel baby blankets. If this were Paris, the women agree, life would be different. Babies would eat together—not out of greasy napkins on the floor of the backseat, but on fine china. The Cockapoos wear jaunty barrettes, and when they see the widows walking toward them in plastic rain hats and raspberry pantsuits, the topknots of the little ones, in unison, begin to quiver.

By the Nape

After she'd fed the workers in my father's garage, my grandmother sank in her rocker to watch her soap opera, As the World Turns, *and when it finished she'd take off her glasses, dab her eyes with Murine, and sleep, her garnet earrings picking up glints of sun that darted under the carriage port and into the living room. Everyone in the house breathed with her, even the parlor relaxed in the deep warmwater sleep of afternoon. I'd honey and bend a slice of bread into a satchel, then sneak out through the summer kitchen, past the chicken coops, the buglevine where the workers came to urinate and smoke cigarettes, past the wide rows of broccoli, eggplant, oysterplant, to the orchard, where I'd curl in the crotch of a sugar pear and dream. The memory of the exact location and the hour of the nectar—birds came draped in cobwebs, butterflies wore pollinia like slippers on their feet. A body grows from its erotic entanglement, and then is reprimanded, as if nature and culture were opposed. Sleeping inside buttery flesh within a dark basement, even a Seckel pip knows the phases of the moon. One could spend a lifetime learning the way a petal grows to accommodate the strength of another body. We were given to ecstasy, my grandmother and I—as she rested from heart failure, she said if you'd slip your arm under me, I think I could dance. We were just the right distance from civilization to be invisible, capable of undergoing transformation. Budded and grafted my sunny side reddened. Happiness lit up the left side of the brain.*

What Makes the Grizzlies Dance

June and finally snowpeas
sweeten the Mission Valley.
High behind the numinous meadows
ladybugs swarm, like huge
lacquered fans from Hong Kong,
like the serrated skirts
of blown poppies,
whole mountains turn red.
And in the blue penstemon
grizzly bears swirl
as they bat snags of color
against their ragged mouths.
Have you never wanted
to spin like that
on hairy, leathered feet,
amid the swelling berries
as you tasted a language
of early summer? Shaping
the lazy operatic vowels,
cracking the hard-shelled
consonants like speckled
insects between your teeth,
have you never wanted
to waltz the hills
like a beast?

Wildcat Path

it would stop, lie down, roll over, playfully clutching at the scanty remains of my dress.
MISS MARY CAMPBELL, York, British Columbia

What if I tell you I walked with a lion
           in the bloody perfume of cottonwood
that flows before the leaves?
           I stepped from a school bus
maybe five o'clock in a black and white
           tricot dress while the young cat
 clicked over rimrock to chase my crinkled shine.
           All my life I've calmed one thing or another,
and half expecting her mother above us
           in the jackpine, I talked while the cat
circled on soft pads beside me, licked my hem.
           Hadn't I always wanted to hike the maple canyon
with my teacher dress in shreds?
           Oh sure I was frightened. Thrilled too.
Falling into a cougar's eyes, yellow stripes
           under cool green, like gooseberries.
Have you heard a wildcat scream?
           Foul breath and baby cry. I wanted to scream
like that every day of my life. Take the world
           with one swipe. Delicate-like, chew on its bones.
Sneak cat. Shadow in the grass.
           My husband watched from the cabin window
as I walked naked down the hill, holding
           my hair with one hand, holding it still
 so the cat would not want it. One shot
           and she lifted over the cutbank, the huckleberry barrens,
the frost-split boulder garden. Neither blood
           nor flesh visible, the only evidence a circle
of hair, a mark where the bullet cut a small aspen.
           My husband chased the cat, saw her by the ditch,
hips high, head low, tail whispering.
           He said she leaped thirty feet before she disappeared.
Next came the neighbormen, their children,
           a biologist with his notebook, ruler, plaster,
a measuring tape. He cast her pugs and tail-drags,
           began to take stories. One man said
he shot a cougar, case-skinned the carcass,
           kept it as a sofa cover till it started flying,

then he threw it, moths and all, into the same river
　　　　　　　where he'd tossed the skull a year earlier.
Everyone thinks I was terrified
　　　　　　　when my husband failed to save me.
I knew all I had to do
　　　　　　　was hold a match to her face,
and that cat would run away.
　　　　　　　I wanted her close. Breathing in my face.
When I serve my family
　　　　　　　at the kitchen table, they lick their lips,
turn toward me—mother, wife, teacher no longer,
　　　　　　　but now the woman who walked with a lion,
and for just the warm scent of my flesh
　　　　　　　and the crackle of a nylon dress, that cat wanted me.
The biologist typed my story, notarized it,
　　　　　　　tried to stash the cat's hair in an envelope, seal it,
but I wear it pressed in a locket covering the faces of my family.
　　　　　　　Nothing else will ever give me such pleasure in my body.

Approaching August

Night takes on its own elegance.
The catenary curve of snakes,
the breathing, pentagonal-shaped flowers,
the shadblow pliant and black with berries.
Orion rises in the east, over fat green
gardens, and all meanness is forgiven.

We canoe the river in the amethyst
hour before dark. Two billion beats
to each heart. Two passengers fish,
two paddle past the chalk caves,
the banks of aster, the flood plains
dense with white tail and beaver.

We are lost near midnight,
a moonless summer evening,
midseason in our senses, midlife.
The sky overhead like glitter ice.
The water round swollen cottonwoods
pulls like tresses and torn paper.

Today I had a letter from France.
What a truly civilized nation,
my friend wrote as she drank her morning coffee
with thick cream in a country café near Avignon.
To my right a man in a black tuxedo sips
raspberry liqueur and soda.

And here on the same latitude
we lie back at dawn on the caving
bank of the Bitterroot. A shadow
slips through the silver grasses.
And then a moth.
And then the moon.

Greenhand

She's crying again,
but all I see are ravens
sparring over a patch
of bloody gravel. The drake's
stood on our creek bank weeks
bleating at her. He tires now,
turns back to his covey
and grain.

She's the saddlemaker's duck.
Since his wife left, the stock
wander loose, ears flattened.
I know the language of this ranch—
barn sour, watcheye, tough as whang leather—
and the saddlemaker teaches me
if you brood it, if it eats from your hand,
it's yours to tend or take for granted.

Saturday morning after pancakes
my friend and I sit around
an oiled table picking
raspberry seeds from our teeth.
Across the creek the mallard paces
in the rain like an old lady,
a dirty blanket tossed over her wings.
They'll eat her soon, he says.

Coyotes. Or beaver.
Or one of those trees they've chewed
to needlepoint'll fall on her.
Smallest wind you hear them crashing.
I wait till dark, freeze coming on fast,
paths like sherbet. Something
in her posture, clip-winged, failure,
that's all too familiar.

Current must have gone
against her. Saddlemaker's horses
follow across the meadow.
They're curious and lonely.

They think I've brought hay.
No moonlight, just the sound
of shore ice cracking, water
pulling through it like a ribbon.

Where the creek divides
I cross an icy log on all fours.
The hen, on a porcelain-thin
piece of ice, garbles to herself.
I toss out feed, and she rises
on dull yellow feet to race
downstream, but the current
slaps her back.

I remember in sixth-grade biology
how we dissected a frog dispassionately
sticking a needle into its brain.
It had starry, excited cells. I mourned
that slimy creature's passing.
I mourned our lack of caring.
When we wrapped its heart in Kleenex
it refused to stop beating.

Minutes I wait shivering for her
to calm, then call again. She flaps
her wings loudly and the island
flutters with hysterical life.
Domestic duck, free from the drake
and the saddlemaker,
she'd rather freeze than take grain
from my green hand.

Half-frozen, I slip back toward the cabin
on a three-toed path. Invisible birds
fly up at me, then wheeze down
from high snags like old men
laughing. Even the night,
with its loud sack of feathers
and sharp curved beak,
digs deeply at my back.

Michael's Wine

Winter again and we want
the same nocturnal rocking,
watching cedar spit
and sketch its leafy flames,
our rooms steamy with garlic
and greasy harvest stew.
Outside frosted windows—
claw marks high on yellow pine,

Venus wobbling in the sky,
the whole valley a glare of ice.
We gather in the kitchen
to make jam from damsons
and blue Italian prunes,
last fruit of the orchard,
sweetest after frost, frothy bushels
steeping in flecked enamel pots.

Michael, our neighbor,
decants black cherry wine,
fruit he ground two years ago,
bound with sugar, then racked
and racked again. It's young and dry.
We toast ourselves, our safety,
time the brandied savory
of late November.

I killed a man this day last year,
says Michael, *while you were away.*
Coming home from town alone,
you know the place in Lolo where the road
curves, where the herd of horses got loose
New Year's Eve, skidded around
white-eyed, cars sliding into them?
Didn't see the man until my windshield broke.

Could have been any one of us.
Twenty-nine years old, half-drunk,
half-frozen. Red and black hunting jacket.
Lucky I was sober. We stand there

plum-stained as Michael's face
fractures into tics and lines.
He strokes his wine red beard.
Michael with no family,

gentle framer's hands, tilts the bottle,
pours a round, as if to toast.
It was so cold, he says,
that when it was over,
he swirls the distilled cherries
under a green lamp, *there was less*
blood on the pavement than you see
this moment in my glass.

Glory Monster

Tipped goblets, the blue heron
flap across the glassy pond.
Two then four they chase each other,
stop at the penciled shoreline
to wrap their necks together.

How like you, Iris, twisting
your green stems in the grasses.
Heron flowers, humid and patient as fists
that spring to flying buttresses,
stained cathedral naves—

if I were to make a monster, Iris,
to chase me, to suffocate in its bloom,
it would be you. Here comes Iris
marching across the pasture, waving
her rapier skirt, twirling

her caterpillar furs. Oh sing
of the brevity of life
and the ephemeral nature of pleasure,
erotic and funereal anguish,
dark-rivered nectar.

Once I lay by a bed of iris
and once by my dying father.
Each time I pressed my face
against the damp
and shriveling flesh.

Thirst

Smack, smack, go our heels on the earth.
We're doing the rain dervish.
We're spinning like wash water.

Rain don't pass over—black
butterflies on singed clover, rasping
popping blond grasshoppers.

See the poplar leaves shake curled baskets,
and the chokecherries slap their limbs
like angry poker players on the grass?

Brassy, recalcitrant sky, we've praised
your suicidal lightning, your skirling robes,
your magenta flowers of scar and blight.

We've lived among cypresses
and singing rats. We know there's
adequate water on the planet.

Our streambed cries for current.
Trout lie, lips pursed, white-eyed,
their flesh spangled with maggots.

Clouds stretch over the tinder forest,
they flirt and roll their moist shoulders.
I remember when I had no lover,

how my every motion was thirst.
I curl beside my husband tonight under the motley sky.
Our bodies rub together, powder like dirt.

Throughout the Duration of a Pulse a Heart Changes Form

Tonight as you return
to our blue sea cottage, see
how the rosewood horse gleams.
I have touched everything.
The white hibiscus
hover against the window,
their red stamens craned like candlewicks.
Winter in this rain-soaked village,
still, the fleshy roses bloom, evenings
sweeten with the smoke of eucalyptus.
I put out a bowl of pecans. I sweep
the white tile floor one, two, three times.
How nervous your absence
makes our friends, as if by marriage
we were blown into a single figurine.
After many weeks alone, we will
turn our simple lives toward
each other. I bathe my limbs carefully.
I perfume the blood beats.
As the yellow spider crawls
into the mouth of the yellow lily
or the butterfly brushes against the blanketflower's eye—
drinks there—so too I've flourished
with each stroke of the body.
Though nights when I could not find
a decent voice on the radio, outside my window
starlings filled the pomegranates, starlings filled the figs.
They ripped open everything. They spit out the seeds.

The Anatomy of Air

Two clouds form, writhe
in animal pleasure
then subside. If color and shape
arise from surface tension alone,
why does a body try
to be entered or embraced?

Michelangelo denied he robbed
the sky's moist palette
though we've each seen altocumulus
boil like a chapel ceiling,
God stretch a finger toward
Adam's contorted body.

The gospel too is air and beautiful.
But philosphers never understood heaven
the mixing of mundane bodies
and neither do I.
Like poplar leaves
I lean into the good weather wind.

When the world is too sharp
I walk toward the canyon
past the bear bait, above
the cracked tectonics, until there's nothing
but glaze, clouds
of meringue and mackeral fat.

Wind slicks back the needles,
and with the world pulled tight as a stocking mask,
smooth as cat skin, beauty's close.
Sadness no more than a hammer blow
broken down, duffled
by the palpitating air.

Flame

When my husband went away
for a season, winter approaching
so fast not even the blaze
of zinnias could keep it back,
he cut and stacked the driest wood,
the most resonant pines of our life.
Slowly he lathered himself with sweat,
with bee swarm and saw grease,
and we leaned together in September's heat
to admire his work, our wealth of grain
and stove lengths. Then the clouds came
scudding down, furry boas, their tails
discarded like icy tissues in clavicles
of rock. When my husband went away
he left me alone in a house about to crack,
knowing that flesh too can freeze,
the spirit turn weak, the hair too thin
for the body, knowing in his absence
those cords would kindle in the silent cabin,
roll and drum like troops, they would be
his bolt of news unfurling, my face flushed red
and red again by the hot inquiring tongues.

Skiing by Moonlight

Gray cloud like a sweater pulled over the heart of the moon.
High-napped purple sky. Why are so many friends
Leaving or getting left behind?

Mao's anti-sparrow campaign: to kill and eat the birds
That were eating the grain. Winter sun drifts away
Leaving thin taffy light. Venus Mercury Jupiter—

Three pearls in the morning sky. By thinking herself
Invisible, the fox walks over hoarfrost not breaking
Morning's delicate lace. Leaving no trace. Lace is beautiful

Because of absence, the place that lets the light through,
Gives it strength. Mother Teresa in the hospital
Watches the annular eclipse. Once every twenty thousand years—

A portion of the sun visible as a ring surrounding the dark moon.
The doctor tells her—protect yourself, hold an X ray of your lungs
Up to the window, let only the waning light pass through.

Fast trail down the mountain -10 degrees. Starving vole
Tracks ornate Victorian filigree. What is the bearing weight
Of an ice crystal ? Why will a person freezing to death

Inch into the false warmth of the moon? Eros is the wound.
White will go to shadblow. White will go to orchid bloom.
Except by nature—as a woman, I will be ungovernable.

The Intricacy of the Song Inverse to the Dull Lores

We learned the song of Swainson's Thrush
as we sat on the deck talking of science
under a comet-littered sky. One rude note
circled us and then the flute. If only we lived
a little higher, deeper in the boreal forest
said the ornithologist, we might hear the Hermit—
nightingale ascending Dvořák's
symphony *From the New World,*
rufous-tailed piano, swamp piccolo.

Why always a fascination with what
is higher, disinclined? Everyone loves a hermit,
be it human or bird, a spare room, a narrow perch.
Behind a cedar hedge, inside a yellow picket fence,
children cluttered as a poet like Rapunzel
from her second-story window bobbed sweetbait
on a string. She would not come down to them,
nor would the utopist under his eaves drinking claret,
taking notes on the grace of pigs, the glaucous seaweed.

Yet even bees drown in their own honey.
No one attends the recluse every day, no one likes
the taciturn one, the inadequate personality.
Vita voluntaria, a life with no fixed rules,
cautioned the saints, leads to degeneration.
Last February a neighbor, called *The Hunch*
for her misshapen body, strung herself
from the cabin rafters. She had been the village crone,
the dried rose in the steamer trunk, long enough.

The way that Alexander Pope dug a melancholy
and brooding hole—studded it with Cornish diamonds,
coral branches, burnished flint, till he turned
the dirt subaqueous—so the world would look
different when he arose, so I too draw the drapes.
Away from humans. Bottle-nosed dolphins

spend 87% of their time at the far end of the pool.
Still they get ulcers in the zoo, balancing all day
on tail fins like ballerinas taking first position.

5.8 acres per human and no species
would go extinct. Scientists say our brains grow larger
not wiser from processing information. Twenty-five
birds in formation fly 70% further than one alone.
If I were a bird, I'd be the Hermit Thrush,
brown and brown again like an old rag rug.
He will not sing on the wintering ground.
He will not sing during migration. He knows
five thousand versions of the same song.

He'll only sing alone near dusk when there is no
competition. Once I rubbed my body
with Mother's vanishing cream till I reeked
and slid with hiding, but you have to be obvious
to make a living. Mockingbirds learn to grind
their gears, to mimic the whine of the freeway,
and even the whisper of a stranger, as it floats
toward an unborn human ear, will register
twenty decibels in the womb.

Spittle Bug

I watched an insect dive
upside down in a crystal bowl.
Magnified, it resembled
a friend's identity crisis—
red eyes, amorphous body
arched like a scorpion.
Probing the water with an iris stem,
I rescued the swimmer,
helped it crawl to the vase lip,
then complimented myself, as if
the bug were my own invention.
It rested on the flower's parchment,
hyperventilating, while I went off
to a day's work. When I returned
it had climbed higher, slathering
purple flesh with froth. Stalled
in one spot like an indulgent head
lost in shampoo, it had taken
the sweet petals with it,
rolling them in babble,
till they were stunted and scabbed.
It looked so harmless at first
roiling in its own spit,
I think I shall call it
gossip bug.

By the Nape

Though sun rubbed honey slow
down rose hips, the world lost
its tenderness. Nipple-haired, joint-swollen,
the grasses waved for attention.
I wanted a watery demonstration for love,
more than wingpaper, twisted stalk of heartleaf.
Squalls rushed over pearling the world,
enlarging the smallest gesture, as I waited
for a drake in first winter plumage
to stretch his neck, utter a grunt whistle,
begin his ritualized display.
I'd held a wild mallard in my palm,
hoodlum heart whooping like a blood balloon.
I'd watched a woman suck coins
between her thighs and up inside her body.
How long she must have trained to let the cold world
enter so. The old man said his neighbor asked him
to milk her breasts, spray the walls, bathe in it.
That was his idea of paradise.
Sometimes I don't know who I am—
my age, my sex, my species—
only that I am an animal who will love
and die, and the soft plumage of another body
gives me pleasure, as I listen for the bubbling
and drumming, the exaggerated drinking
of a lover rising vertically from the sedges
to expose the violet streaks inside his body,
the vulnerable question of a nape.

Golden-Mantled Ground Squirrel

Obsequious. You come begging
outside my screen. Sidelong
you stare all morning.
I know that greeting.
It's the same as mine.

You can't make up your flimsy mind.
Do you like the world better—
distant or direct? Little Beckett
shifting chicles from one nervous cheek
to the other, will you never seek more

than safe passage? If I so much as breathe,
you convulse like water on hot grease.
Relax, no one cares about you.
If you left the territory next Friday
for good, there'd be no party.

That's the privilege of being discreet.
You know the warm dens,
the sound of your solitary beat
against the walls,
and those strawberries

ripening under my porch,
the ones no hand can reach?
They're yours—
deep maroon, reclusive,
they smell so sweet.

To Touch with a Smoothing Iron

Yellow with water stains,
wine, carpet-beetle droppings,
sweat in, cried in, just plain tired—
I have taken an old dress,
washed it, and wet
spread it on the grass.

Like the nervous bird
inside my chest
that I must breathe
to life each morning,
it comes back
moist smelling.

Yellow jacket on snowberry,
how happy we are
this morning, he rubs his feet
against the pink blossom,
flies upside down
at the same time.

Trajectory

The ice dam broke, slabs
jamming a cabin overland,
its faithful dog
locked inside, yelping.

My friend told me a boy jumped
the ice floe, floated for miles
through slithery red mudstone,
trout-skinned shale.

I rode the telling—
it felt like love, not familial,
but of the body, moving fast,
out of control.

We'd raced one night, my friend and I,
while we sucked black cherries.
Silent but for snapshackles.
A dozen white sails.

The body seeks abandon—
somewhere in the limbics,
the cortex, the tangible feel
of being alive.

I'd flown too close
to cropland once, almost crashed
against the soil's water-stained satin.
Einfülung, we become

the moving figure
as it rivers and freezes,
the skin responds, the heart
and eye, we empathize.

I'd watched a blind dog
find a ball by sniffing

where it bounced,
rebounded off a wall.

How magnificent
the circuits of the brain,
how the absence of an object
leaves a scent,

a line of trajectory
for even a blind spaniel to follow.
When Search and Rescue reached
the boy by flowing ice,

they wanted to tie a life jacket on him,
wanted to find his parents
to take him home. He said he wanted
to be left alone.

They threatened to arrest him.
He had long skinny arms and a sharp face,
which he turned away.
The ice floated to the opposite shore,

the boy stepped off, walked
into the forest. No one knew
if he survived, if anyone
ever saw him again.

Imagine careening slick water,
over peamouths and shiners
on a punky boat of ice, like orbiting
the planet on a tempered glass

windshield, one crash
and all would shatter, not shatter exactly,
but fracture full spectrum, like life
as we know it—radiant, beyond rescue.

Woodpecker

On the day the poppies
burst their tight green fists,
and the geum and the geranium
bloomed all bloody red
and ruby, so the pileated
woodpecker returned.

He ricocheted off the pine trunk,
then picking among yellow bugs
sped quickly to the pea vines.
Fat-breasted, he drilled his name,
let it drip and trill round the forest,
down his throat,

landlord of the mountain,
mafioso in a tweed vest,
red-crested whale of the sky,
he announced the summer solstice.
We ran to the window knowing
at last snow would melt on the Bitterroots

to flood our fields, knowing
it was time for aurora borealis,
heaven's beast, her tentacles
flicking like jellyfish
on the shortest
night of the year.

We did the dance of the woodpecker,
the fat flicker, the pagan priest,
when clover bloomed, salsify
and wild roses, and we knew
that winter was over, we did the dance
of the smart, hardheaded,

flashy creatures of the world.
After all, in summer when blood
is thick and dark as the flicker's crest,
when we might all fatten on berries

and weeds alone, isn't there room
for each of us, even the greedy ones?

After all, have you never wanted
to drive at top speed,
to slam into a tree or dive
from a ledge or catch fire
or slit your wrists
and let the fluids geyser?

Not suicide, but its burning,
not rage directed at humankind—no,
the heart remains a sweet berry and ripe.
But red drives the stickleback
wild, red small spots among the green,
among the brown rocks.

And so on the long day
of the summer solstice
when the world spins
silly with light, we do
the dance of the woodpecker,
twirling our skirts

and mustaches, tapping
our resonant branches,
our underwear flashing white,
as we shake the irregular flags
of our body into
undulant, raw flight.

SANDRA ALCOSSER's collection of poems, *Except by Nature*, was chosen by Eamon Grennan for the 1997 National Poetry Series. Her first book, *A Fish to Feed All Hunger*, was selected by James Tate as the Associated Writing Programs' Award Series Winner in Poetry; *Sleeping Inside the Glacier*, an artist collaboration, has just been published by Brighton Press. Alcosser has received numerous honors including two National Endowment for the Arts Fellowships; her poems have been published widely in journals including the *American Poetry Review*, the *New Yorker*, the *Paris Review*, *Poetry*, the *Pushcart Prize Series*, and the *Yale Review*. She lives in Florence, Montana, and teaches in the graduate writing program at San Diego State University.

This book was designed by Will Powers. It is set in ITC New Baskerville and Gill Sans type by Stanton Publication Services, Inc., and manufactured by BookCrafters on acid-free paper.

The Baskerville typeface was first cut in the 1750s by John Baskerville, of Birmingham England. This early "transitional" typeface caused a furor when first introduced; readers complained that it "sparkled" too much. Its descendants have since become some of the most widely used typefaces. Gill Sans is among the most noted "humanist" sans serif types, designed by Eric Gill in Britain in 1928.